PROSPER YOURSELF WITH FAITH!

YOUR POWERFUL DAILY COMPANION
FOR ATTRACTING WEALTH!

CICELY BLAND

FOREWORD BY CHARLES FILLMORE
The Twelve Powers of Man

Prosper Yourself with Faith:

Your Powerful Daily Companion for Attracting Wealth

Published by Empower House Publishing

222 Broadway

19th Floor

New York, NY 10038

www.empowerhousepublishing.com

Library of Congress Cataloging-in-Publication Data

Bland, Cicely

Prosper Yourself with Faith / by Cicely Bland

ISBN-13: 978-0-9816573-3-2 (trade paperback)

1. Self-help/Prosperity/Inspirational I. Title

Library of Congress Control Number: 2016931134

DEDICATION

This book is dedicated to everyone who has ever uttered positive words to me or about me and prayed faithfully for my wellbeing. I am grateful.

FOREWORD

SPIRITUAL POWER OF FAITH

Faith words should be expressed both silently and audibly. The power of the spoken word is but slightly understood, because the Law of the Word is not rightly observed. The Word is the creative idea in Divine Mind, which may be expressed by man when he has fulfilled the Law of Expression.

All words are formative but not all words are creative. The creative word lays hold of Spirit substance and power. Physical science hints at this inner substance and energy, in its description of the almost inconceivable power inherent in the universal ether. We are told that the manifest forces, such as heat, light, and electricity, are but faint manifestations of an omnipresent element which is thousands of times greater than these weak expressions.

Radio is opening up a new field of activity in the use of the spoken word. A newspaper article on the wireless telephone says:

Do you happen to know that a single word spoken in Lower Broadway, New York, among the skyscrapers, could break every pane of glass in adjacent buildings and create a disturbance that would be felt for a mile in every direction?

The human voice, transformed into electrical energy for wireless transmission, develops 270 horse power. The power of ten men is equal to one horse power. The human voice electrified for wireless purposes is equivalent to the power of 2,700 men. In the various processes that step up a voice for radio transmission across the Atlantic ocean, it becomes 135,000 times more powerful than when uttered by the person sending the message.

Thus, starting with an initial energy of 1/1,000 of an electric watt, the voice is boosted by a powerful station until it is intensified 100 million times.

If the spoken word can be mechanically intensified a hundred million times, how much greater will be its power when energized by Spirit! When Jesus said with a loud voice to Lazarus, "Come forth," He must have made contact with the creative word referred to in the 1st chapter of John, because the results showed its life-giving character. When He healed the centurion's servant by His word sent forth on invisible currents, He said that the work was done through faith.

So faith must boost the spoken word even more than a hundred million times, as evidenced by its marvelous results. That the word of faith has an inner force, and that this force rushes forth and produces remarkable transformations in the phenomenal world, is the testimony of thousands who have witnessed its results.

Jesus said: "If ye have faith as a grain of mustard seed, ye shall say unto this mountain, Remove hence to yonder place; and it shall remove; and nothing shall be impossible unto you." He knew about the great spiritual machinery that the word of faith sets into action. He illustrated how man spiritually developed could by faith control the elements, quell storms, walk on water, retard or increase the growth of life and substance in grains, trees, animals, and men.

Charles Fillmore
~"The Twelve Powers of Man"

MESSAGE FROM THE AUTHOR

A lot can be said about good habits of daily personal hygiene. We bathe, brush our teeth and groom ourselves so that we can feel our very best and not offend others when we are in social settings. Hopefully, we are equally concerned about mental, spiritual and emotional hygiene as well.

We should never neglect practicing a daily routine of habitually thinking positive thoughts in order to manifest our highest good and greatest joy in every area of our lives. In order to clean up any negative suggestions or ideas that our minds are exposed to throughout each day, we use daily affirmations: positive statements of Truth.

The Prosper Yourself with Faith book, along with the other books in The Twelve Powers of Prosperity Series, provides powerful affirmations to be used for your deliberate creation of great success, wealth, health and relationships. Use these affirmations daily with purposeful repetition.

I have taught dozens of success and prosperity courses in schools, spiritual centers and business organizations and have found that the use of affirmations is indeed one of the most effective ways of programming our minds for the good that we desire.

In Napoleon Hill's classic prosperity book "Think and Grow Rich", he writes, "Repetition of affirmation of orders to your subconscious mind is the only known method of the voluntary development of the emotion of faith."

Therefore, use this book, along with the other titles in The Twelve Powers of Prosperity series, to increase your total wellbeing using your God-given spiritual faculties. Each affirmation helps to develop, cultivate and discipline your spiritual powers. You can move from glory to glory by continuously using your powerful mind in an optimistic and positive way.

Speak your Prosper Yourself with Faith affirmations aloud or repeat them to yourself silently throughout the day. Create "prosperity circles" with family, friends, classmates, colleagues and members of your spiritual community. It is always helpful to use the extraordinary power of collective intention when working with affirmations. Give the book series to loved ones or others you desire to see grow more wealthy and successful. Share your daily Prosper Yourself with Faith affirmations with others via text, email or social media. The more the merrier!

~CICELY BLAND

INTRODUCTION

"Now faith is the substance of things hoped for, the evidence of things not seen" Heb. 11:1. In order to understand the purpose and function of Faith, we must consider the nature of God. God is all good. The source of everything spiritual and material, but the source is invisible. Faith is our ability to draw from the invisible realm into visible expression.

Faith is unshakeable certainty that what you believe will come to pass. The Bible teaches us to walk by faith and not by sight. This means that outer appearances or circumstances can be overlooked as we look within us to the Universal Source of all creation to supply everything that we need.

We are always using our Faith faculty to some degree whether we realize it or not. Faith is also pivotal and being fearful is using our faculty of Faith erroneously.

We become more receptive to Spirit when we place more confidence in the "within" than in the "without" as all our faculties move from within us into the external realm. Let us always remember to place our Faith in God's order, in God's law and in unchanging grace. Let us be thankful to God for our faculty of Faith.

As we exercise our faith, we strengthen our faith. We exercise our faith by eliminating negative thinking. We center our minds only on God's best for us knowing that it will come to pass with ease and in perfect ways.

Faith sees a way when there appears to be no way. Faith sees opportunities arise out of so-called problems. We have all been given a measure of faith. The Bible teaches us that faith the size of a mustard seed can remove mountains from our paths. Is your faith at least the size of a mustard seed? If so, celebrate the Infinite Power you possess and claim your victory by the authority of the Creator of the universe!

AFFIRMATIONS

HOW TO PROSPER YOURSELF WITH FAITH AFFIRMATIONS

- Each day, read your Faith affirmation aloud along with the supporting passage and scripture. A great time to do this is when you first wake up in the morning. This will help to consciously set your intention on attracting prosperity throughout the day.

- After your daily reading, attempt to quiet yourself for several minutes and think on the Faith affirmation that you have just read. Notice any feeling of resistance to the new thought that you are dwelling upon. Past programming and conditioning may resurface as you are consistently adding new, healthier thoughts of abundance and prosperity to your mind.

- It is very helpful to write down thoughts and feelings each day as you work with your Faith affirmations. Also, write down inspirations and ideas that come to you.

- You may be divinely led to take some type of action. If so. Do not resist the guidance that you receive. Act upon it!

- Throughout the day, focus on and repeat, aloud or silently, your daily Faith affirmations. Be aware and grateful of new avenues of prosperity that open for you as a result of your new way of thinking.

- It is helpful to reread your daily Faith affirmation along with the supporting passage and scripture before you go to bed at night. Give thanks for all evidence that new prosperity is blossoming in your life and will continue to manifest in your future as a reward for changing your thinking. This is also a good time for journaling your thoughts and ideas.

MY FAITH CLEARS THE WAY FOR GREAT THINGS TO HAPPEN!

God's abundance can flow to you in infinite ways. First, you must be open and receptive to receive the magnificent things that God has in store for you. Fear and doubt create blocks to the flow of good into your life experience. Clear the way for great things to happen by applying faith to every area of your life.

AFFIRM: My faith clears the way for great things to happen. I am open and receptive to the flow of infinite abundance and absolute good. I release all fear and doubt and quickly remove any blocks to my highest good and greatest joy. I believe God has magnificent things in store for me. By my faith, the way has been made clear.

Verily, verily, I say unto you, He that believeth on me, the works that I do shall he do also; and greater works than these shall he do; because I go unto my Father.
John 14:12 (KJV)

I GIVE MY FULL ATTENTION TO FAITH!

Our faith is the foundation upon which every area of our life is built. We can allow ourselves to be distracted from faith when we face the demands of life. By giving our full attention to faith, we direct our energy to the solution, not the challenge. See the world through faith-filled eyes knowing that God's will is always good and perfect. All of our perceived problems are divinely solved when we activate our faith in every situation.

AFFIRM: I give my full attention to faith. My life is built upon a strong foundation of faith. I direct my energy only on the solution and away from the challenges. I see the world through the eyes of God and know it is all good and very good. I activate my faith in every situation and expect Divine solutions.

Trust in the LORD and do good. Then you will live safely in the land and prosper.
Psalm 37:3 (NLT)

I BELIEVE IN MIRACLES!

When we see others facing challenges, we should remind them they are children of God. They are not facing the situation alone. God is always present. As believers, we have the responsibility to encourage and empower others with our words, thoughts and actions. We can use our faith as a beacon when another is trapped in the darkness of fear and doubt.

AFFIRM: I encourage and empower others! I am grateful to be a believer in God as the only power and presence in existence. I know that God is always present and I share that truth with others. I remind them of the Infinite power of the Holy Spirit and the availability of that power to all humanity. I am a beacon of light to others during their time of darkness.

For there is one body and one Spirit, just as you have been called to one glorious hope for the future.
Ephesians 4:4 (NLT)

BLESSINGS FLOW ENDLESSLY FROM GOD'S FOUNTAIN OF GOOD!

Imagine a world with no worries, no mistakes and no accidents. That world is possible for all of us to achieve, if we turn our consciousness to the grace and goodness of God. Psalm 23:6 ensures us that goodness and mercy shall follow us all the days of our lives. Believe this! There is no need to chase the good you desire. When you are aware of your oneness with the Creator, you will attract everything that serves your highest good and greatest joy.

AFFIRM: Blessings flow endlessly from God's fountain of good. I release all worries. I trust in the grace and goodness of God. I believe God's promise that goodness and mercy will surely follow me for the rest of my life. Using my faith makes life much easier! My oneness with the Creator makes it possible for me to attract the good I desire.

Surely goodness and mercy shall follow me all the days of my life: and I will dwell in the house of the LORD for ever.
Psalm 23:6 (KJV)

I STARVE FEAR
WITH FAITH!

When faced with challenges, we have a tendency to allow fearful thoughts to reign in our minds. Doubts and uncertainties clutter our thoughts and begin to choke out the voice of Spirit. This is a great opportunity to apply faith to the situation. Starve fearful, pessimistic thoughts with ideas full of faith and optimism.

AFFIRM: I starve fear with faith. When faced with challenges, I flood my experiences with positive thoughts. I release doubts and uncertainties and clear the mental clutter that does not serve my highest good and greatest joy. I have faith that everything is and will always be fantastic.

The Lord is my light and my salvation; whom shall I fear? The LORD is the strength of my life; of whom shall I be afraid?
Psalm 27:1 (KJV)

I SEE BEYOND APPEARANCES!

God is limitless. We are heirs to the limitless good of the Creator of all. See beyond appearances. See only abundance instead of lack. See only perfect health as a possibility for yourself. See yourself living your dreams and know that your limitless God supports you every step of the way.

Affirm: I see beyond appearances. I am a limitless heir to all that God is and has. I see only abundance. I see only perfect health. I see only the highest good and greatest joy for myself and the entire world.

I TRUST THE LORD WITH ALL MY HEART!

Put no trust in worldly things or people. People may disappoint you. Material things can be broken, lost or stolen. Circumstances change constantly. God never changes. God's love is eternal. It is time we center ourselves with the will of the Creator and trust Divine Guidance.

AFFIRM: I trust the Lord with all my heart. I recognize God alone as the Source of all things visible. Therefore, I rely only on God for my good. I never put my trust in worldly things alone. Instead, I center myself with the will of the Creator and trust Divine guidance.

The LORD redeemeth the soul of his servants: and none of them that trust in him shall be desolate.
Psalm 34:22 (KJV)

I ACTIVELY PRACTICE FAITH IN EVERY AREA OF MY LIFE!

Wouldn't it be fantastic if we were able to let go of stress and worry? Fear breeds stress, worry, doubt, guilt, anger and inner conflict. Faith breeds confidence, assurance, patience, courage, peace, harmony and balance. Choose to exercise the power of faith in all you do and experience. The results are amazing!

Affirm: I actively practice faith in every area of my life. I surrender all skepticism and rely solely on God for a life filled with joy. I gladly let go of stress, doubt and worry caused by fear-based thinking. My thoughts are centered in the faith that I am one with the true and living God.

"I and the Father are one."
John 10:30 (NASB)

FAITH HAS RESTORED MY SOUL!

Any time you feel disconnected within, it is a chance to remind yourself of your oneness with the Creator of the universe. This will keep your soul alert and aware of the presence of Infinite Intelligence. Awaken from your soul sleep! Faith the size of a mustard seed or a grain of sand can remove the largest mountain from your path.

Affirm: Faith has restored my soul. I am connected to the Divine Source of all good. My soul is alert, awakened and in tune with Infinite Intelligence. I remind myself daily of my oneness with the Creator of the universe. My faith grows stronger with each passing day.

Create in me a clean heart, O God;
and renew a right spirit within me.
Psalm 51:10 (KJV)

MOUNTAIN, GET OUT OF MY WAY!

You can speak your good into existence. With the power of your spoken word, you can cast any obstacle out of your life. Jesus teaches us that it only takes faith the size of a mustard seed to move mountains out of our way. What apparent mountain are you facing? A mountain of debt and unpaid bills? A mountain of work that needs to be done? Know that faith activates the universe to work everything out in your favor. Say boldly, "Mountain, get out of my way!"

AFFIRM: Mountain, get out of my way! I believe in the power of my spoken word. I combine my positive words with thoughts of faith. I know my unshakeable faith in Spirit activates the universe to work everything out in my favor. There is no mountain high enough to keep my good away from me.

"You don't have enough faith," Jesus told them.
"I tell you the truth, if you had faith even as small as a mustard seed, you could say to this mountain, 'Move from here to there,' and it would move. Nothing would be impossible."
Matthew 17:20 (NLT)

BY MY FAITH, I AM HEALED!

Do you desire a healing in any area of your life? A financial healing? A relationship healing? A healing of your physical body? Christ says, "According to your faith, be it unto you." Instead of worrying, believe the situation to be healed and watch the healing manifest!

AFFIRM: By my faith, I am healed. I give thanks to God for my healing. Every area of my life is perfect. I have perfect finances. I have perfect health. My relationships are filled with peace and harmony. I choose to stop worrying and believe in God to heal every situation I may encounter.

I EMANCIPATE MYSELF FROM WITHIN!

Who can keep you in bondage if you know that you can free yourself from within? No one! God is your deliverance and defense. Nothing or no one can keep you in bondage without your permission. We create bondage experiences with bondage thinking. Take back any power you have given to external authority and emancipate your mind!

AFFIRM: I emancipate myself from within. I free myself from the shackles of bondage thinking. Nothing or no one can confine my limitless Spirit. I take back all power I have given away due to limited thinking. My mind is renewed and I choose to experience absolute freedom.

For the law of the Spirit of life in Christ Jesus hath made me free from the law of sin and death.
Romans 8:2 (KJV)

FAITH IS MY SWORD AND SHIELD!

In the Bible, when David was preparing to face Goliath, he went forth with no physical armor. Instead, he girded himself with the full armor of God. Although he was a young boy at the time, David knew that faith was all he needed to defeat the giant. How are you facing the giants in your life? With fear or faith?

AFFIRM: Faith is my sword and shield. I am divinely protected by the full armor of God. With my faith, I easily defeat the seeming "giants" in my life experiences. I am more than a conqueror through Christ which strengthens me. Spirit within me wins all my battles.

The LORD is my strength and shield. I trust him with all my heart. He helps me, and my heart is filled with joy. I burst out in songs of thanksgiving.
Psalm 28:7 (NLT)

I AM OBEDIENT TO GOD'S INSTRUCTIONS!

The Bible is filled with stories of the faithful who were obedient to God and were greatly rewarded. Abraham became the father of many nations because of his faith. Noah followed God's instruction for building an ark that would protect him and all his descendents from destruction. We must be willing to obey the guidance and instructions of Holy Spirit even if we do not immediately understand why.

AFFIRM: I am obedient to God's instructions. I listen and obey even if I do not understand why at that moment. God knows what is best for me. Where I am led by Spirit, I will follow. My faith protects me from destruction when the storms of life appear.

For the Scriptures tell us, "Abraham believed God, and God counted him as righteous because of his faith."
Romans 4:3 (NLT)

I CAN DO ALL THINGS THROUGH CHRIST WHO STRENGHTHENS ME!

Have you ever talked yourself out of a good idea because of fear? Fear of ridicule? Fear of a lack of resources? God has not given you a spirit of fear. Move towards your goals boldly and confidently. Trust that everything you need has already been provided by the Divine!

Affirm: I can do all things through Christ who strengthens me. I am fearless. My ideas are gifts from God. I trust that all the resources I need to manifest my ideas are being provided. I move toward my goals with boldness and confidence!

I can do all things through Christ who strengthens me.
Philippians 4:13 (KJV)

MY LIFE IS A REFLECTION OF FAITH!

Look around you and see your life for what it really is. Your life is a reflection of your faith. Every person has been given their own measure of faith. Christ said, "By your faith you are healed." If you desire a change in any area of your life, apply faith to the situation and believe in the perfect outcome.

Affirm: My life is a reflection of my faith. I have faith that life is good and very good. I have faith that God is always with me. With my abundant measure of faith, I can heal any circumstance despite appearances. I first apply faith to all areas of my life and watch with amazement as perfect results unfold!

Understand, therefore, that the LORD your God is indeed God. He is the faithful God who keeps his covenant for a thousand generations and lavishes his unfailing love on those who love him and obey his commands.
Deuteronomy 7:9 (KJV)

SPIRIT HAS ALL THE RIGHT ANSWERS!

Overcome self doubt and inner conflict with the awareness that Spirit has all of the right answers. What does that mean? It means that you can completely relax when you have absolute trust in God. Tap into the Spirit within you! You make the best decisions when you allow yourself to be divinely guided.

AFFIRM: Spirit has all the right answers. I know everything I need to know. I relax and trust the power within me to determine my good. I am tapped into Spirit. My decisions are divinely guided.

And this is the confidence that we have in him, that, if we ask any thing according to his will, he heareth us: And if we know that he hear us, whatsoever we ask, we know that we have the petitions that we desired of him.
1 John 5:14-15 (KJV)

I AM FAITH IN ACTION!

How often do we say we have faith and when confronted with a challenge we are filled with doubt and fear? Activate your faith in the midst of what appears to be a crisis. Focus on the power within you to overcome whatever you face. Let faith be your first reaction.

AFFIRM: I am faith in action. I turn all challenges over to the power within me. I activate my faith and expect to see everything unfold perfectly in my life. I see beyond appearances and know that God is the answer.

I AM WORTHY OF ABSOLUTE GOOD!

It is God's will that all of us live healthy, happy and prosperous lives. God loves us fully and completely. It does not matter what you have done in the past. You deserve only the best. It is time to release guilt, anger, resentment and any other fear-based thought. Decide that you are absolutely worthy and deserving of all that is good simply because you are a child of God. Accept your divine inheritance.

AFFIRM: I am worthy of absolute good. God loves me and desires for me to have the best of everything. It does not matter what I have done or said in the past. I release all thoughts rooted in fear and choose to experience good from now throughout eternity. I am worthy of perfect health, love and finances. I gratefully accept my divine inheritance of good. Thanks, God. And so it is!

The thief's purpose is to steal and kill and destroy. My purpose is to give them a rich and satisfying life.
John 10:10 (NLT)

I AM FEARLESS, FAITHFUL AND FREE!

Free will is God's most precious gift to humans. God is pleased when you fearlessly and faithfully align your will with Spirit and exercise your will despite the judgment or opinions of others. God has a Divine Plan for your life. Once God has revealed your purpose to you, get moving!

AFFIRM: I am fearless, faithful and free! I am aware that God has a Divine Plan for me. I refuse to submit my free will to the opinions or judgments of others! No weapon formed against me shall prosper. I move along my destined path with a fearless heart and a faithful spirit.

O love the LORD, all you His godly ones!
The LORD preserves the faithful And fully
recompenses the proud doer.
Psalm 31:23 (NASB)

I AM
A WINNER!

We can beat all of the odds when we believe in our hearts that we are winners. God has given us a spirit of power that can declare victory over any circumstance. You cannot fail when you adopt the attitude of a champion.

Affirm: I am a winner! I beat all of the odds. I overcome all boundaries. I defeat all enemies. I declare victory in all of my affairs. I have the mind of a champion!

For whoever is born of God triumphs over the world;
and this is the victory which conquers the world,
even our faith.
1 John 5:4 (Lamsa)

I HAVE FAITH IN THE BEST OUTCOMES!

Do you have faith that the best will happen or fear the worst? Overcome all pessimistic thoughts with the faith that your ideas will manifest at the appointed time. Work toward achieving optimum results. God's power is your power and you are quite capable of producing stellar accomplishments!

AFFIRM: I have faith in the best outcomes. I release the need to anticipate the worst scenarios. I overcome pessimism with optimism. I have faith that my ideas are manifesting in Divine time. I work toward achieving optimum results in every area of my life. I tap into the power of faith to produce the best outcomes today and always.

Now all glory to God, who is able, through his mighty power at work within us, to accomplish infinitely more than we might ask or think.
Ephesians 3:20 (NLT)

I OVERCOME CHALLENGES WITH FAITH!

Challenges are cleverly disguised opportunities. We create challenges in order to grow and progress into what we are destined to be. If you are not careful, challenges can also distract you from your Divine purpose. Confront challenges with faith knowing that the grace of God is on your side.

AFFIRM: I overcome challenges with faith. I recognize challenges as opportunities for my growth and progression. I refuse to allow challenges to distract me from my Divine purpose. Instead, I confront all challenges with faith knowing that God handles all things on my behalf in perfect order. I desire. For this, I give thanks.

The LORD is my rock, my fortress, and my savior; my God is my rock, in whom I find protection. He is my shield, the power that saves me, and my place of safety.
Psalm 18:2 (NLT)

I HAVE FAITH
IN MY SAFETY
AND SECURITY!

There is no need to fear any impending danger or misfortune. God loves you and keeps you safe and protected at all times. It does not matter that others are trying to convince you of possible threats to your safety. These negative messages only rob you of joy and peace of mind. Instead, saturate your mind with thoughts of security. Have faith that every area of your life will unfold perfectly.

AFFIRM: I have faith in my safety and security. All of my surroundings are protected by the light and love of God. I forgive others who attempt to convince me that impending dangers threaten me. I know that God loves me. I keep my mind focused on Spirit and have faith that I am always dwelling in the safety of Divine protection.

In peace I will lie down and sleep, for you alone,
O LORD, will keep me safe.
Psalm 4:8 (NLT)

DIVINE FAITH EMPOWERS ME!

Those of us who are seeking empowerment should begin our search within. Too often, we tend to look outside of ourselves for the answers that will bring us the greatest fulfillment. If we begin to shift our focus from the external to the internal, we will quickly realize that applying faith to situations resolves them in perfect and Divine ways

Affirm: Divine Faith empowers me. I look within for my empowerment. My power of faith guides me to make all of the right choices. My power of faith heals every area of my life. My power of faith prospers me abundantly. As I shift my focus from the external to the internal, I apply my faith and see all situations resolved in perfect and divine ways.

This Good News tells us how God makes us right in his sight. This is accomplished from start to finish by faith. As the Scriptures say, "It is through faith that a righteous person has life."
Romans 1:17 (NLT)

HAVING FAITH FEELS GOOD!

Many people feel as though faith is something that one must strain to obtain. Yet, faith is a natural power, a natural ability. We all have been given our own measure of faith. The faith you have is more than enough for you to manifest your highest dreams. What will you activate your faith to accomplish?

AFFIRM: Having faith feels good. I do not have to strain to obtain more faith. Faith is my natural power. Faith is my natural ability. I activate my faith to manifest prosperity in every area of my life. I have faith that I can experience a superb life filled with amazing moments!

Cling to your faith in Christ, and keep your conscience clear.
1 Timothy 1:19 (NLT)

I AM PROSPERED BY MY FAITH!

There is no scarcity in the realm of God. When you put your faith in the Creator of all, you are being faithful to the belief that there is infinite abundance available to you. Believe that you can have what you want to have. Believe that you can do what you want to do. Believe that you can go where you want to go. Believe that you can be who you want to be. It will be done unto you according to your faith.

AFFIRM: I am prospered by my faith. I put my faith in the Creator of all things. I faithfully believe that there is infinite abundance always available for me. I believe that I can have what I want to have. I believe that I can do what I want to do. I believe that I can go where I want to go. I also believe that I can be who I want to be. I give thanks for the prosperity that I generate by my right use of my faith.

Now someone may argue, "Some people have faith; others have good deeds." But I say, "How can you show me your faith if you don't have good deeds? I will show you my faith by my good deeds."
James 2:18 (NLT)

I HAVE
FAITH IN
FORGIVENESS

Forgiveness is one of the fastest and most harmonious vehicles to use to create the prosperity that you desire. Every grudge that you mentally and emotionally resolve will free you to experience a consistent flow of blessings. Refusing to forgive will hinder and block the flow of your good to you. In fact, lack of forgiveness will repel your good away from you. Instead, feel the joy, peace and comfort that come with allowing old wounds to finally heal and true forgiveness to take place.

AFFIRM: I have faith in forgiveness. I know that forgiveness is the fastest and most harmonious vehicle to use to create the prosperity that I desire. I now mentally and emotionally resolve all grudges. I forgive everything and everyone that could possibly need forgiving. All of my good is now freely flowing in my direction. I feel the joy, peace and comfort that come with allowing old wounds to finally heal and forgiveness to take place.

*And forgive us our debts, as we also have
forgiven our debtors.
Matthew 6:12 (NASB)*

MY FAITH GROWS STRONGER AND STRONGER EVERY DAY!

Your faith can only diminish if you allow it to do so. Conversely, your faith grows stronger through continuous use and discipline. Your faith may be tested if you are confronted with a challenge. Will you allow the challenges of life to weaken your faith or will you allow your faith to grow stronger by using your inner power to overcome them? It is your choice.

AFFIRM: My faith grows stronger and stronger every day. I do not allow my faith to be diminished. I use my faith in all areas of my life. I apply my strong faith when I am confronted with challenges. As a result, my faith grows stronger and challenges are resolved perfectly. I am grateful that I can depend on stronger faith as time progresses.

Test yourselves to see if you are in the faith; examine yourselves! Or do you not recognize this about yourselves, that Jesus Christ is in you-- unless indeed you fail the test?
2 Corinthians 13:5 (NASB)

I FOCUS ONLY ON DESIRED RESULTS!

Whatever you choose to focus on will expand your mind and experiences. On what do you focus? Do you focus on lack? Abundance? Do you place most of your attention on challenges or God's power within you? Focus only on what you desire to see manifest in your life. Keep your eyes on the prize!

AFFIRM: I focus only on desired results. I know what I choose to focus on will expand in my experience. I focus on unlimited abundance in every area of my life. I focus on the will and way of the divine presence of God. I meet all challenges boldly by keeping my eyes on the prize!

Finally, brethren, whatever is true, whatever is honorable, whatever is just, whatever is pure, whatever is lovely, whatever is gracious, if there is any excellence, if there is anything worthy of praise, think about these things.
Philippians 4:8 (RSV)

JOURNAL QUESTIONS TO CONSIDER

(Use provided pages and/or your own journals/notebooks)

Today, I demonstrated Faith by: _______________________

____

____

____

I missed my opportunity to demonstrate Faith when: __________

____

____

____

Tomorrow, I have Faith I will: _______________________

____

____

____

JOURNAL QUESTIONS TO CONSIDER

(Use provided pages and/or your own journals/notebooks)

Today, I demonstrated Faith by: _______________________

____

____

____

I missed my opportunity to demonstrate Faith when: _________

____

____

____

Tomorrow, I have Faith I will: _______________________

____

____

____

JOURNAL QUESTIONS TO CONSIDER

(Use provided pages and/or your own journals/notebooks)

Today, I demonstrated Faith by: ________________________

____

____

____

I missed my opportunity to demonstrate Faith when: __________

____

____

____

Tomorrow, I have Faith I will: ________________________

____

____

____

JOURNAL QUESTIONS TO CONSIDER

(Use provided pages and/or your own journals/notebooks)

Today, I demonstrated Faith by: ___________________________

____

____

____

I missed my opportunity to demonstrate Faith when: _________

____

____

____

Tomorrow, I have Faith I will: ___________________________

____

____

____

JOURNAL QUESTIONS TO CONSIDER

(Use provided pages and/or your own journals/notebooks)

Today, I demonstrated Faith by: __________________

____

____

____

I missed my opportunity to demonstrate Faith when: __________

____

____

____

Tomorrow, I have Faith I will: __________________

____

____

____

JOURNAL QUESTIONS TO CONSIDER

(Use provided pages and/or your own journals/notebooks)

Today, I demonstrated Faith by: _______________________

____

____

____

I missed my opportunity to demonstrate Faith when: _________

____

____

Tomorrow, I have Faith I will: _______________________

____

____

____

JOURNAL QUESTIONS TO CONSIDER

(Use provided pages and/or your own journals/notebooks)

Today, I demonstrated Faith by: ______________________________

____

____

____

I missed my opportunity to demonstrate Faith when: __________

____

____

____

Tomorrow, I have Faith I will: ______________________________

____

____

____

JOURNAL QUESTIONS TO CONSIDER

(Use provided pages and/or your own journals/notebooks)

Today, I demonstrated Faith by: ___________________________

____

____

____

I missed my opportunity to demonstrate Faith when: _________

____

____

Tomorrow, I have Faith I will: ____________________________

____

____

____

GRATITUDE PAGES

(Use provided pages and/or your own journals/notebooks)

I am so joyful and thankful now that: _______________

____

____

____

Today, I am grateful for: _______________

____

____

____

I am giving faithful thanks in advance for: _______________

____

____

____

GRATITUDE PAGES

(Use provided pages and/or your own journals/notebooks)

I am so joyful and thankful now that: _______________________

____

____

____

Today, I am grateful for: _______________________________

____

____

____

I am giving faithful thanks in advance for: _______________

____

____

____

GRATITUDE PAGES

(Use provided pages and/or your own journals/notebooks)

I am so joyful and thankful now that: _______________________

____

____

____

Today, I am grateful for: _______________________________

____

____

____

I am giving faithful thanks in advance for: _________________

____

____

____

GRATITUDE PAGES

(Use provided pages and/or your own journals/notebooks)

I am so joyful and thankful now that: ___________________

____

____

____

Today, I am grateful for: ___________________

____

____

____

I am giving faithful thanks in advance for: ___________________

____

____

____

GRATITUDE PAGES

(Use provided pages and/or your own journals/notebooks)

I am so joyful and thankful now that: ___________________

____

____

____

Today, I am grateful for: ___________________________

____

____

____

I am giving faithful thanks in advance for: _____________

____

____

____

GRATITUDE PAGES

(Use provided pages and/or your own journals/notebooks)

I am so joyful and thankful now that: ______________________

____

____

____

Today, I am grateful for: ______________________________

____

____

I am giving faithful thanks in advance for: ______________

____

____

____

GRATITUDE PAGES

(Use provided pages and/or your own journals/notebooks)

I am so joyful and thankful now that: _______________________

____

____

____

Today, I am grateful for: _______________________________

____

____

____

I am giving faithful thanks in advance for: _______________

____

____

____

GRATITUDE PAGES

(Use provided pages and/or your own journals/notebooks)

I am so joyful and thankful now that: _______________________

____

____

____

Today, I am grateful for: _______________________________

____

____

____

I am giving faithful thanks in advance for: _______________

____

____

____

NOTES

NOTES

NOTES

NOTES

NOTES

NOTES

NOTES

NOTES

NOTES

NOTES

ORDER FORM

Mail with check/money order enclosed or credit card information to:
Empower House Publishing, LLC
222 Broadway, 19th Floor
New York, NY 10038

Fax to: 1-888-208-4317

Qty	Title	Price	
	Prosper Yourself with Faith	$9.99 x PER BOOK	
	U.S. Shipping	$3.99 x PER BOOK	
		Total	

Order online now at www.empowerhousepublishing.com. **PayPal**™

❑ Check /Money Order   ❑ Visa   ❑ MasterCard   ❑ American Express

____
Card Number

____
Security Code (CVV2, CVC2, CID)

____
Expiration Date

____
Signature

Ship to: _______________________

____

____

____

Prosper Yourself with Faith is available at special quantity discounts for bulk purchase for sales promotions, fundraising and educational needs. Special books or book excerpts also can be created to fit specific needs. For details, write Empower House Publishing, Special Markets, 222 Broadway, 19th Floor, New York, NY 10038 or email info@empowerhousepublishing.com.

Prosper Yourself with Faith!

Book Design by Emmanuel Okoye
Editing by Phyllis Armstrong and Marilyn Coates